Book 1
Python Programming In A Day
BY SAM KEY

&

Book 2
PHP Programming Professional Made Easy
BY SAM KEY

Book 1
Python Programming In A Day

BY SAM KEY

*Beginners Power Guide To Learning
Python Programming From Scratch*

Programming Box Set #39: Python Programming in a Day & PHP Programming Professional Made Easy

Table Of Contents

Introduction

I want to thank you and congratulate you for purchasing the book, "Python Programming in a Day: Beginners Power Guide To Learning Python Programming From Scratch".

This book contains proven steps and strategies on how you can program using Python in a day or less. It will contain basic information about the programming language. And let you familiarize with programming overall.

Python is one of the easiest and most versatile programming languages today. Also, it is a powerful programming language that is being used by expert developers on their complex computer programs. And its biggest edges against other programming languages are its elegant but simple syntax and readiness for rapid application development.

With python, you can create standalone programs with complex functionalities. In addition, you can combine it or use it as an extension language for programs that were created using other programming languages.

Anyway, this eBook will provide you with easy and understandable tutorial about python. It will only cover the basics of the programming language. On the other hand, the book is a good introduction to some basic concept of programming. It will be not too technical, and it is focused on teaching those who have little knowledge about the craft of developing programs.

By the way, take note that this tutorial will use python 3.4.2. Also, most of the things mentioned here are done in a computer running on Microsoft Windows.

Thanks again for purchasing this book. I hope you enjoy it!

Chapter 1: Getting Prepared

In developing python scripts or programs, you will need a text editor. It is recommended that you use Notepad++. It is a free and open source text editor that you can easily download and install from the internet. For you to have the latest version, go to this link: http://notepad-plus-plus.org/download/v6.6.9.html.

Once you install Notepad++ and you are ready to write python code lines, make sure that you take advantage of its syntax-highlighting feature. To do that, click on Language > P > Python. All python functions will be automatically highlighted when you set the Language to python. It will also highlight strings, numbers, etc. Also, if you save the file for the first time, the save dialog box will automatically set the file to have an extension of .py.

To be able to run your scripts, download and install python into your computer. The latest version, as of this writing, is 3.4.2. You can get python from this link: https://www.python.org/download.

And to be able to test run your python scripts in Notepad++, go to Run > Run... or press the F5 key. A small dialogue box will appear, and it will require you to provide the path for the compiler or a program that will execute your script. In this case, you will need to direct Notepad++ to the python executable located in the installation folder.

By default or if you did not change the installation path of python, it can be found on the root folder on the drive where your operating system is installed. If your operating system is on drive C of your computer, the python executable can be found on C:\Python34\python.exe. Paste that line on the dialogue box and add the following line: $(FULL_CURRENT_PATH). Separate the location of the python.exe and the line with a space, and enclosed the latter in double quotes. It should look like this:

C:\Python34\python.exe "$(FULL_CURRENT_PATH)"

Save this setting by pressing the Save button in the dialogue box. Another window will popup. It will ask you to name the setting and assign a shortcut key to it. Just name it python34 and set the shortcut key to F9. Press the OK button and close the dialogue box. With that setting, you can test run your program by just pressing the F9 key.

By the way, if the location you have set is wrong, the python executable will not run. So to make sure you got it right, go to python folder. And since you are already there, copy python.exe, and paste its shortcut on your desktop. You will need to access it later.

And you are all set. You can proceed on learning python now.

Chapter 2: Interactive Mode – Mathematical Operations

Before you develop multiple lines of code for a program, it will be best for you to start playing around with Python's interactive mode first. The interactive mode allows a developer to see immediate results of what he will code in his program. For new python users, it can help them familiarize themselves on python's basic functions, commands, and syntax.

To access the interactive mode, just open python.exe. If you followed the instructions in the previous chapter, its shortcut should be already on your desktop. Just open it and the python console will appear.

Once you open the python executable, a command console like window will appear. It will greet you with a short message that will tell you the version of python that you are using and some command that can provide you with various information about python. At the bottom of the message, you will the primary prompt (>>>). Beside that is the blinking cursor. In there, you can just type the functions or commands you want to use or execute. For starters, type credits and press Enter.

Mathematical Operations in Interactive Mode

You can actually use the interactive mode as a calculator. Try typing 1 + 1 and press Enter. Immediately after you press the Enter, the console provided you with the answer to the equation 1 + 1. And then it created a new line and the primary prompt is back.

In python, there are eight basic mathematical operations that you can execute. And they are:

- Addition = 1 + 1

- Subtraction = 1 − 1

- Multiplication = 1 * 1

Programming Box Set #39: Python Programming in a Day & PHP Programming Professional Made Easy

- Division = 1 / 1

In older versions of Python, if you divide integers and the division will result to a decimal, Python will only return an integer. For example, if you divide 3 by 2, you will get 1 as an answer. And if you divide 20 by 39, you will get a zero. Also, take note that the result is not rounded off. Python will just truncate all numbers after the decimal point.

In case you want to get an accurate quotient with decimals, you must convert the integers into floating numbers. To do that, you can simply add a decimal point after the numbers.

- Floor Division = 1 // 1

If you are dividing floating numbers and you just want to get the integer quotient or you do not want the decimals to be included, you can perform floor division instead. For example, floor dividing 5.1515 by 2.0 will give you a 2 as an integer quotient.

- Modulo = 1 % 1

The modulo operator will allow you to get the remainder from a division from two numbers. For example, typing 5 % 2 will give you a result of 1 since 5 divided by two is 2 remainder 1.

- Negation = -1

Adding a hyphen before a number will make it a negative number. You can perform double, triple, or multiple negations with this operator. For example, typing -23 will result into -23. Typing --23 will result into 23. Typing -----23 will result into -23.

- Absolute Value = abs(1)

When this is used to a number, the number will be converted to its absolute value or will be always positive. For example, abs (-41) will return 41.

Python calculates equation using the PEMDAS order, the order of operations that are taught in Basic Math, Geometry, and Algebra subjects in schools. By the way, PEMDAS stands for Parentheses, Exponents, Multiplication, Division, Addition, and Subtraction.

Chapter 3: Interactive Mode – Variables

During your Math subject when you were in grade or high school, your teacher might have taught you about variables. In Math, variables are letters that serve as containers for numbers of known and unknown value. In Python or any programming language, variables are important. They act as storage of values. And their presence makes the lives of developers easy.

However, unlike in school, variables in programming languages are flexible when it comes to their names and functions. In Python, variables can have names instead of a single letter. Also, they can also contain or represent text or strings.

Assigning Values to Variables

Assigning a value to a variable is easy in Python. You can just type the name of your variable, place an equal sign afterwards, and place the value you want to be contained or stored in the variable. For example:

```
>>> x = 151
```

When you assign a value in a variable, Python will not reply any message. Instead, it will just put your cursor on the next primary prompt. In the example, you have assigned the value 151 to the variable x. To check if it worked, type x on the console and press Enter. Python will respond with the value of the variable x.

Just like numbers, you can perform arithmetical operations with variable. For example, try typing x – 100 in the console and press Enter. Python will calculate the equation, and return the number 51 since 151 – 100 = 51. And of course, you can perform mathematical operations with multiple variables in one line.

By the way, in case that you did not define or assign a value to a new variable, Python will return an error if you use it. For example, if you try to subtract x with y, you will get an error that will say name 'y' is not defined. You received that message since you have not assigned anything to the variable y yet.

In addition, you can assign and change the value of a variable anytime. Also, the variable's value will not change if you do not assign anything to it. The variable and its value will stay in your program as long as you do not destroy it, delete it, or close the program.

To delete a variable, type del then the name of the variable. For example:

>>> del x

Once you try to access the variable again by typing its name and pressing Enter after you delete it, Python will return an error message saying that the variable is not defined.

Also, you can assign calculated values to a variable. For example:

>>> z = 1 + 4

If you type that, type z, and press Enter, Python will reply with 5. Variables are that easy to manipulate in Python.

You can also assign the value of one variable to another. Below is an example:

>>> y = 2

>>> z = y

The variable z's value will be changed to 2.

Chapter 4: Interactive Mode – Strings

Your program will not be all about numbers. Of course, you would want to add some text into it. In Python, you can do that by using strings. A string or string literal is a series of alphanumeric numbers or characters. A string can be a word or sentence. A lone character can be also considered as a string. To make your program display a string, you will need to use the print function. Below is an example on how to use it:

>>> print ("Dogs are cute.")

To display a string using the print function properly, you will need to enclose the string with parentheses and double quotations. Without the parentheses, you will receive a syntax error. Without the quotes, Python will think that you are trying to make it display a variable's value.

By the way, in older versions of Python, you can use print without the parentheses. However, in version 3 and newer, print was changed to as a function. Because of that, it will require parentheses.

For example:

>>> print ("Dogs")

That line will make Python print the word or string Dogs. On the other hand:

>>> print (Dogs)

That line will return a variable not defined error. With that being said, you can actually print or display the content of a variable. For example:

>>> x = 14

>>> print (x)

The print function will display the number 14 on the screen. By the way, you can also use single quotes or even triple single or double quotes. However, it is recommendable to use a single double for those who are just started in program development.

Assigning Strings to Variables

Assigning strings to variables is easy. And it is the same as assigning numbers to them. The only difference is that you will need to enclose the string value in double quotations or reverse commas as some developers call them. For example:

>>> stringvariable = "This is a string."

If you type stringvariable in the interactive mode console, it will display the This is a string text. On the other hand, if you do this:

>>> print (stringvariable)

Python will print the string, too.

Strings can include punctuation and symbols. However, there are some symbols or punctuations that can mess up your assignment and give you a syntax error. For example:

>>> samplestring = "And he said, "Hi.""

In this case, you will get a syntax error because the appearance of another double quote has appeared before the double quote that should be enclosing the string. Unfortunately, Python cannot recognize what you are trying to do here. Because of that, you need the by escaping the string literal.

To escape, you must place the escape character backslash (\) before the character that might produce conflict. In the example's case, the characters that might produce a syntax error are the two double quotes inside. Below is the fixed version of the previous paragraph:

>>> samplestring = "And he said, \"Hi.\""

Writing the string assignment like that will not produce an error. In case you print or type and enter the variable samplestring in the console, you will see the string that you want to appear, which is And he said, "Hi.".

Escape Sequences in Python

Not all characters are needed to be escaped. Due to that, the characters that you can escape or the number of escape sequences are limited. Also, escape sequences are not only for preventing syntax errors. They are also used to add special characters such as new line and carriage return to your strings. Below is a list of the escape sequences you can use in Python:

- \\ = Backslash (\)

- \" = Double quote (")

- \' = Single quote (')

- \b = Backspace

- \a = ASCII Bell

- \n = Linefeed

- \f = Formfeed

- \t = Horizontal Tab

- \r = Carriage Return

- \v = ASCII Vertical Tab

Preventing Escape Sequences to Work

There will be times that the string that you want to print or use might accidentally contain an escape sequence. Though, it is a bit rare since the backslash character is seldom used in everyday text. Nevertheless, it is still best that you know how to prevent it. Below is an example of an escape sequence that might produce undesirable results to your program:

>>> print ("C:\Windows\notepad.exe")

When Python processes that, you might encounter a problem when you use since the \n in the middle of the string will break the string. For you to visualize it better, below is the result:

>>> print ("C:\Windows\notepad.exe")

C:\Windows

otepad.exe

>>> _

To prevent that you must convert your string to a raw string. You can do that by placing the letter r before the string that you will print. Below is an example:

>>> print (r"C:\Windows\notepad.exe")

C:\Windows\notepad.exe

>>> _

Basic String Operations

In Python, you can perform operations on your strings. These basic string operations also use the common arithmetical operators, but when those operators are used on strings, they will produce different results. There are two of these. And they use the + and * operators. Below are examples on how to use them:

>>> print ("cat" + "dog")

catdog

>>> print ("cat" * 3)

catcatcat

>>> _

When the + operator is used between two strings, it will combine them. On the other hand, if the multiplication operator is used, the string will be repeated depending on the number indicated.

By the way, you cannot use operators between strings and numbers – with the exception of the multiplication symbol. For example:

>>> variable_x = 1 + "text"

The example above will return an unsupported operand type since Python does not know what to do when you add a string and a number.

Chapter 5: Transition from Interactive Mode to Programming Mode

Alright, by this time, you must already have a good feel on Python's interactive mode. You also know the basic concepts of variables, strings, and numbers. Now, it is time to put them together and create a simple program.

You can now close Python's window and open Notepad++. A new file should be currently opened once you open that program. The next step is to set the Language setting into Python. And save the file. Any name will do as long that you make sure that your file's extension is set to .py or Python file. In case the save function does not work, type anything on the text file. After you save it, remove the text you typed.

Now, you will start getting used to programming mode. Programming mode is where program development start. Unlike interactive mode, programming mode requires you to code first, save your file, and run it on Python. To get a feel of the programming mode, copy this sample below:

print ("Hello World!")

print ("This is a simple program that aims to display text.")

print ("That is all.")

input ("Press Enter Key to End this Program")

If you followed the instructions on the Getting Prepared chapter, press the F9 key. Once you do, Python will run and execute your script. It will be read line by line by Python just like in Interactive mode. The only difference is that the primary prompt is not there, and you cannot input any command while it is running.

Input Function

On the other hand, the example code uses the input function. The input function's purpose is to retrieve any text that the user will type in the program and wait for the Enter key to be pressed before going to the next line of code below it. And when the user presses the key the program will close since there are no remaining lines of code to execute.

By the way, if you remove the input function from the example, the program will just print the messages in it and close itself. And since Python will process those lines within split seconds, you will be unable to see if it work. So, in the following examples and lessons, the input function will be used to temporarily pause your scripts or prevent your program to close prematurely.

You can use the input function to assign values to variables. Check this example out:

```
print ( "Can you tell me your name?" )

name = input("Please type your name: ")

print ( "Your name is " + name + ".")

print ( "That is all." )

input ( "Press Enter Key to End this Program. \n" )
```

In this example, the variable name was assigned a value that will come from user input through the input function. When you run it, the program will pause on the Please type your name part and wait for user input. The user can place almost anything on it. And when he presses enter, Python will capture the text, and store it to variable name.

Once the name is established, the print function will confirm it and mention the content of the name variable.

Programming Box Set #39: Python Programming in a Day & PHP Programming Professional Made Easy

Data Type Conversion

You can also use the input function to get numbers. However, to make sure the program will understand that its numbers that it will receive, make sure that your input does not include non-numeric characters. Below is a sample code of an adding program:

```
print ( "This program will add two numbers you would input." )

first_number = input ( "Type the first number: " )

second_number = input ( "Type the second number: " )

sum = int(first_number) + int(second_number)

print ( "The sum is " + str(sum) )

input ( "Press Enter Key to End this Program. \n" )
```

In this example, the program tries to get numbers from the user. And get the sum of those two numbers. However, there is a problem. The input function only produces string data. That means that even if you type in a number, the input will still assign a string version of that number to the variable.

And since they are both strings, you cannot add them as numbers. And if you do add them, it will result into a joined string. For example, if the first number was 1 and the second number was 2, the sum that will appear will be 12, which is mathematically wrong.

In order to fix that, you will need to convert the strings into its numeric form. In this example, they will be converted to integers. With the help of the int function, that can be easily done. Any variable will be converted to integer when placed inside the int function.

So, to get the integer sum of the first_number and second_number, both of them were converted into integers. By the way, converting only one of them will result into an error. With that done, the sum of the two numbers will be correctly produced, which 3.

Now the second roadblock is the print function. In the last print function, the example used an addition operator to join the The sum is text and the variable sum. However, since the variable sum is an integer, the operation will return an error. Just like before, you should convert the variable in order for the operation to work. In this case, the sum variable was converted to a string using the str function.

There are other data types in Python – just like with other programming languages. This part will not cover the technicalities of those data types and about the memory allocation given to them, but this part is to just familiarize you with it. Nevertheless, below is a list of a few of the data type conversion functions you might use while programming in Python:

- Long() – converts data to a long integer

- Hex() – converts integers to hexadecimal

- Float() – converts data to floating-point

- Unichr() – converts integers to Unicode

- Chr() – converts integers to characters

- Oct() – converts integers to octal

Chapter 6: Programming Mode – Conditional Statements

Just displaying text and getting text from user are not enough for you to make a decent program out of Python. You need your program to be capable of interacting with your user and be capable of producing results according to their inputs.

Because of that, you will need to use conditional statements. Conditional statements allow your program to execute code blocks according to the conditions you set. For you to get more familiar with conditional statements, check the example below:

```
print ( "Welcome to Guess the Number Game! " )

magic_number = input ( "Type your guess: " )

if ( magic_number  == "1" ):

    print ( "You Win!" )

else:

    print ( "You Lose!" )

input ( "Press enter to exit this program " )
```

In this example, the if or conditional statement is used. The syntax of this function differs a bit from the other functions discussed earlier. In this one, you will need to set a conditional argument on its parentheses. The condition is that if the variable magic_number is equal to 1, then the code block under it will run. The colon after the condition indicates that it will have a code block beneath it.

When you go insert a code block under a statement, you will need to indent them. The code block under the if statement is print ("You Win!"). Because of that, it is and should be indented. If the condition is satisfied, which will happen if the user entered 1, then the code block under if will run. If the condition was not satisfied, it will be ignored, and Python will parse on the next line with the same indent level as if.

That next line will be the else statement. If and else go hand in hand. The have identical function. If their conditions are satisfied, then the program will run the code block underneath them. However, unlike if, else has a preset condition. Its condition is that whenever the previous conditional statement is not satisfied, then it will run its code block. And that also means that if the previous conditional statement's condition was satisfied, it will not run.

Due to that, if the user guesses the right magic number, then the code block of if will run and the else statement's code block will be ignored. If the user was unable to guess the right magic number, if's code block will be ignored and else's code block will run.

Conclusion

Thank you again for purchasing this book!

I hope this book was able to help you to understand the basic concepts of programming and become familiar in Python in just one day.

The next step is to research and learn looping in Python. Loops are control structures that can allow your program to repeat various code blocks. They are very similar to conditional statements. The only difference is that, their primary function is to repeat all the lines of codes placed inside their codeblocks. Also, whenever the parser of Python reaches the end of its code block, it will go back to the loop statement and see if the condition is still satisfied. In case that it is, it will loop again. In case that it does not, it will skip its code block and move to the next line with the same indent level.

In programming, loops are essential. Truth be told, loops compose most functionalities of complex programs. Also, when it comes to coding efficiency, loops makes program shorter and faster to develop. Using loops in your programs will reduce the size of your codes. And it will reduce the amount of time you need to write all the codes you need to achieve the function you desire in your program.

If you do not use loops in your programs, you will need to repeat typing or pasting lines of codes that might span to hundreds of instances – whereas if you use loops in your programs, those hundred instances can be reduced into five or seven lines of codes.

There are multiple methods on how you can create a loop in your program. Each loop method or function has their unique purposes. Trying to imitate another loop method with one loop method can be painstaking.

On the other hand, once you are done with loops, you will need to upgrade your current basic knowledge about Python. Research about all the other operators that were not mentioned in this book, the other data types and their quirks and functions, simple statements, compound statements, and top-level components.

To be honest, Python is huge. You have just seen a small part of it. And once you delve deeper on its other capabilities and the possible things you could create with it, you will surely get addicted to programming.

Finally, if you enjoyed this book, please take the time to share your thoughts and post a review on Amazon. We do our best to reach out to readers and provide the best value we can. Your positive review will help us achieve that. It'd be greatly appreciated!

Thank you and good luck!

Book 2
PHP Programming Professional Made Easy

By Sam Key

Expert PHP Programming Language Success in a Day for any Computer User!

Table of Contents

Introduction

I want to thank you and congratulate you for purchasing the book, "Professional PHP Programming Made Easy: Expert PHP Programming Language Success in a Day for any Computer User!"

This book contains proven steps and strategies on how to quickly transition from client side scripting to server side scripting using PHP.

The book contains a condensed version of all the topics you need to know about PHP as a beginner. To make it easier for you to understand the lessons, easy to do examples are included.

If you are familiar with programming, it will only take you an hour or two to master the basics of PHP. If you are new to programming, expect that you might take two to three days to get familiar with this great server scripting language.

Thanks again for purchasing this book, I hope you enjoy it!

Chapter 1: Setting Expectations and Preparation

PHP is a scripting language primarily used by web developers to create interactive and dynamic websites. This book will assume that you are already familiar with HTML and CSS. By the way, a little bit of XML experience is a plus.

This book will also assume that you have a good understanding and experience with JavaScript since most of the explanations and examples here will use references to that client side scripting language

To be honest, this will be like a reference book to PHP that contains bits of explanations. And since JavaScript is commonly treated as a prerequisite to learning PHP, it is expected that most web developers will experience no difficulty in shifting to using this server side scripting language.

However, if you have little knowledge of JavaScript or any other programming language, expect that you will have a steep learning curve if you use this book. Nevertheless, it does not mean that it is impossible to learn PHP without a solid background in programming or client side scripting. You just need to play more with the examples presented in this book to grasp the meaning and purpose of the lessons.

Anyway, unlike JavaScript or other programming languages, you cannot just test PHP codes in your computer. You will need a server to process it for you. There are three ways to do that:

1. Get a web hosting account. Most web hosting packages available on the web are PHP ready. All you need to do is code your script, save it as .php or .htm, upload it to your web directory, and access it.

2. Make your computer as simple web server. You can do that by installing a web server application in your computer. If your computer is running on Microsoft Windows, you can install XAMPP to make your computer act like a web server. Do not worry. Your computer will be safe since your XAMPP, by default, will make your computer only available to your use.

3. Use an online source code editor that can execute PHP codes. Take note that this will be a bit restricting since most of them only accept and execute PHP codes. It means that you will not be able to mix HTML, CSS, JavaScript, and PHP in one go. But if you are going to study the basics, which the lessons in this book are all about, it will be good enough.

Chapter 2: PHP Basics

This chapter will teach you the primary things that you need to know when starting to code PHP. It includes PHP's syntax rules, variables, constants, echo and print, operators, and superglobals.

Syntax

PHP code can be placed anywhere in an HTML document or it can be saved in a file with .php as its file extension. Just like JavaScript, you will need to enclose PHP code inside tags to separate it from HTML. The tag will tell browsers that all the lines inside it are PHP code.

PHP's opening tag is <?php and its closing tag is ?>. For example:

```
<!DOCTYPE html>
</html>
<head></head>
<body>
        <h1>Heading for the page</h2>
        <p>Some paragraph</p>
        <?php
                // Insert some PHP code in here.
        ?>
</body>
</html>
```

Echo and Print

PHP code blocks do not only return the values you requested from them, but you can also let it return HTML or text to the HTML file that invoked the PHP code blocks. To do that, you will need to use the echo or print command. Below are samples on how they can be used:

```
<?php
echo "Hello World!";
?>
<?php
print "Hello World!";
?>
```

Once the browser parses that part of the HTML, that small code will be processed on the server, and the server will send the value "Hello World" back to the client. Browsers handle echo and print values by placing them in the HTML file code. It will appear after the HTML element where the PHP code was inserted. For example:

```php
<p>This is a paragraph.</p>
<?php
echo "Hello World!";
?>
<p>This is another paragraph.</p>
```
Once the browser parses those lines, this will be the result:

This is a paragraph.

Hello World!

This is another paragraph.

You can even echo HTML elements. For example:
```php
<p>P1.</p>
<?php
print "<a href='http://www.google.com' >Google</a>";
?>
<p>P2.</p>
```
As you have witnessed, both echo and print have identical primary function, which is to send output to the browser. They have two differences however. Print can only handle one parameter while echo can handle multiple parameters. Another difference is that you can use print in expressions since it returns a value of 1 while you cannot use echo. Below is a demonstration of their differences:

```php
<?php
echo "Hello World!", "How are you?";
?>
<?php
print "Hello World!", "How are you?";
?>
```
The echo code will be successfully sent to the client, but the print code will bring up a syntax error due to the unexpected comma (,) and the additional parameter or value after it. Though, if you want to use print with multiple parameters, you can concatenate the values of the parameters instead. String concatenation will be discussed later.

```php
<?php
$x = 1 + print("test");
echo $x;
?>
<?php
$x = 1 + echo("test");
echo $x;
?>
```
The variable $x will have a value of 2 since the expression print("test") will return a value of 1. Also, even it is used as a value in an expression, the print command will still produce an output.

On the other hand, the echo version of the code will return a syntax error due to the unexpected appearance of echo in the expression.

Many web developers use the echo and print commands to provide dynamic web content for small and simple projects. In advanced projects, using return to send an array of variables that contain HTML content and displaying them using JavaScript or any client side scripting is a much better method.

Variables

Creating a variable in JavaScript requires you to declare it and use the keyword var. In PHP, you do not need to declare to create a variable. All you need to do is assign a value in a variable for it to be created. Also, variables in PHP always starts with a dollar sign ($).

```
<?php
$examplevariable = "Hello World!";
echo $examplevariable;
?>
```

There are rules to follow when creating a variable, which are similar to JavaScript's variable syntax.

➤ The variable's name or identifier must start with a dollar sign ($).

➤ An underscore or a letter must follow it.

➤ Placing a number or any symbol after the dollar sign instead will return a syntax error.

➤ The identifier must only contain letters, numbers, or underscores.

➤ Identifiers are case sensitive. The variable $x is treated differently from $X.

You can assign any type of data into a PHP variable. You can store strings, integers, floating numbers, and so on. If you have experienced coding using other programming languages, you might be thinking where you would need to declare the data type of the variable. You do not need to do that. PHP will handle that part for you. All you need to do is to assign the values in your variables.

Variable Scopes

Variables in PHP also change their scope, too, depending on the location where you created them.

Local

If you create a variable inside a function, it will be treated as a local variable. Unlike JavaScript, assigning a value to variable for the first time inside a function will not make them global due to way variables are created in PHP.

Global

If you want to create global variables, you can do it by creating a value outside your script's functions. Another method is to use the global keyword. The global keyword can let you create or access global variables inside a function. For example:

```
<?php
function test() {
     global $x;
     $x = "Hello World!";
}
test();
echo $x;
?>
```

In the example above, the line global $x defined variable $x as a global variable. Because of that, the echo command outside the function was able to access $x without encountering an undefined variable error.

As mentioned a while ago, you can use the global keyword to access global variables inside functions. Below is an example:

```
<?php
$x = "Hello Word!";
function test() {
     global $x;
     echo $x;
}
test();
?>
```

Just like before, the command echo will not encounter an error as long as the global keyword was used for the variable $x.

Another method you can use is to access your script's global values array, $GLOBALS. With $GLOBALS, you can create or access global values. Here is the previous example used once again, but with the $GLOBALS array used instead of the global keyword:

```
<?php
function test() {
     $GLOBALS['x'] = "Hello World!";
}
test();
echo $x;
?>
```

Take note that when using $GLOBALS, you do not need the dollar sign when creating or accessing a variable.

Static

If you are not comfortable in using global variables just to keep the values that your functions use, you can opt to convert your local variables to static. Unlike local variables, static variables are not removed from the memory once the function that houses them ends. They will stay in the memory like global variables, but they will be only accessible on the functions they reside in. For example:

```php
<?php
function test() {
        static $y = 1;
        if (empty($y))
                {$y = 1;}
        echo $y . " ";
        $y += $y;
}
test();
test();
test();
test();
test();
?>
```

In the example, the variable $y's value is expected to grow double as the function is executed. With the help of static keyword, the existence and value of $y is kept in the script even if the function where it serves as a local variable was already executed.

As you can see, together with the declaration that the variable $y is static, the value of 1 was assigned to it. The assignment part in the declaration will only take effect during the first time the function was called and the static declaration was executed.

Superglobals

PHP has predefined global variables. They contain values that are commonly accessed, define, and manipulated in everyday server side data execution. Instead of manually capturing those values, PHP has placed them into its predefined superglobals to make the life of PHP programmers easier.

- ➢ **$GLOBALS**

- ➢ **$_SERVER**

- ➢ **$_REQUEST**

- ➢ **$_POST**

- ➢ **$_GET**

➢ **$_FILES**

➢ **$_ENV**

➢ **$_COOKIE**

➢ **$_SESSION**

Superglobals have CORE USES IN PHP SCRIPTING. YOU WILL BE MOSTLY USING ONLY FIVE OF THESE SUPERGLOBALS IN YOUR EARLY DAYS IN CODING PHP. THEY ARE: $GLOBALS, $_SERVER, $_REQUEST, $_POST, AND $_GET.

Constants

Constants are data storage containers just like variables, but they have global scope and can be assigned a value once. Also, the method of creating a constant is much different than creating a variable. When creating constants, you will need to use the define() construct. For example:

```
<?php
define(this_is_a_constant, "the value", false);
?>
```

The define() construct has three parameters: define(name of constant, value of the constant, is case sensitive?). A valid constant name must start with a letter or an underscore – you do not need to place a dollar sign ($) before it. Aside from that, all other naming rules of variables apply to constants.

The third parameter requires a Boolean value. If the third parameter was given a true argument, constants can be accessed regardless of their case or capitalization. If set to false, its case will be strict. By default, it will be set to false.

Operators

By time, you must be already familiar with operators, so this book will only refresh you about them. Fortunately, the usage of operators in JavaScript and PHP is almost similar.

➢ Arithmetic: +, -, *, /, %, and **.

➢ Assignment: =, +=, -=, *=, /=, and %=.

➢ Comparison: ==, ===, !=, <>, !==, >, <, >=, and <=.

➢ Increment and Decrement: ++x, x++, --x, and x--.

➢ Logical: and, or, xor, &&, ||, and !.

➢ String: . and .=.

➢ Array: +, ==, ===, !=, <>, and !==.

Chapter 3: Flow Control

Flow control is needed when advancing or creating complex projects with any programming language. With them, you can control the blocks of statements that will be executed in your script or program. Most of the syntax and rules in the flow control constructs in PHP are almost similar to JavaScript, so you will not have a hard time learning to use them in your scripts.

Functions

Along the way, you will need to create functions for some of the frequently repeated procedures in your script. Creating functions in PHP is similar to JavaScript. The difference is that function names in PHP are not case sensitive. For example:

```php
<?php
function test($parameter = "no argument input") {
      print $parameter;
}
TEST("Success!");
tEsT();
?>
```

In JavaScript, calling a function using its name in different casing will cause an error. With PHP, you will encounter no problems or errors as long as the spelling of the name is correct.

Also, did you notice the variable assignment on the sample function's parameter? The value assigned to the parameter's purpose is to provide a default value to it when the function was called without any arguments being passed for the parameter.

In the example, the second invocation of the function test did not provide any arguments for the function to assign to the $parameter. Because of that, the value 'no argument input' was assigned to $parameter instead.

In JavaScript, providing a default value for a parameter without any value can be tricky and long depending on the number of parameters that will require default arguments or parameter values.

Of course, just like JavaScript, PHP functions also return values with the use of the return keyword.

If, Else, and Elseif Statements

PHP has the same if construct syntax as JavaScript. To create an if block, start by typing the if keyword, and then follow it with an expression to be evaluated inside parentheses. After that, place the statements for your if block inside curly braces. Below is an example:

```php
<?php
$color1 = "blue";
if ($color1 == "blue") {
        echo "The color is blue! Yay!";
}
?>
```

If you want your if statement to do something else if the condition returns a false, you can use else.

```php
<?php
$color1 = "blue";
if ($color1 == "blue") {
        echo "The color is blue! Yay!";
}
else {
        echo "The color is not blue, you liar!";
}
?>
```

In case you want to check for more conditions in your else statements, you can use elseif instead nesting an if statement inside else. For example:

```php
<?php
$color1 = "blue";
if ($color1 == "blue") {
        echo "The color is blue! Yay!";
}
else {
        if ($color == "green") {
                echo "Hmm. I like green, too. Yay!";
        }
        else {
                echo "The color is not blue, you liar!";
        }
}
?>
```

Is the same as:

```php
<?php
$color1 = "blue";
if ($color1 == "blue") {
        echo "The color is blue! Yay!";
}
elseif ($color == "green" {
        echo "Hmm. I like green, too. Yay!";}
else {
        echo "The color is not blue, you liar!";
}
?>
```

Using elseif is less messy and is easier to read.

Switch Statement

However, if you are going to check for multiple conditions for one expression or variable and place a lot of statements per condition satisfied, it is better to use switch than if statements. For example, the previous if statement is the same as:

```php
<?php
$color1 = "blue";
switch ($color1) {
        case "blue":
                echo "The color is blue! Yay!";
                break;
        case "green":
                echo "Hmm. I like green, too. Yay!";
                break;
        case default:
                echo "The color is not blue, you liar!";
}
?>
```

The keyword switch starts the switch statement. Besides it is the value or expression that you will test. It must be enclosed in parentheses.

Every case keyword entry must be accompanied with the value that you want to compare against the expression being tested. Each case statement can be translated as if <expression 1> is equal to <expression 2>, and then perform the statements below.

The break keyword is used to signal the script that the case block is over and the any following statements after it should not be done.

On the other hand, the default case will be executed when no case statements were satisfied by the expression being tested.

Chapter 4: Data Types – Part 1

PHP also has the same data types that you can create and use in other programming languages. Some of the data types in PHP have different ways of being created and assigned from the data types in JavaScript.

Strings

Any character or combination of characters placed in double or single quotes are considered strings in PHP. In PHP, you will deal with text a lot more often than other programming languages. PHP is used typically to handle data going from the client to the server and vice versa.   Due to that, you must familiarize yourself with a few of the most common used string operators and methods.

Numbers

Integer

Integers are whole numbers without fractional components or values after the decimal value. When assigning or using integers in PHP, it is important that you do not place blanks and commas between them to denote or separate place values.

An integer value can be positive, negative or zero. In PHP, you can display integers in three forms: decimal (base 10), octal (base 8), or hexadecimal (base 16). To denote that a value is in hexadecimal form, always put the prefix 0x (zero-x) with the value (e.g., 0x1F, 0x4E244D, 0xFF11AA). On the other hand, to denote that a value is in octal form, put the prefix 0 (zero) with the value (e.g., 045, 065, and 0254).

If you echo or print an integer variable, its value will be automatically presented in its decimal form. In case that you want to show it in hexadecimal or octal you can use dechex() or decoct() respectively. For example:

```
<?php
echo dechex(255);
echo decoct(9);
?>
```
The first echo will return FF, which is 255 in decimal. The second echo will return 11, which is 9 in octal. As you might have noticed, the prefix 0x and 0 were not present in the result. The prefixes only apply when you write those two presentations of integers in your script.

On the other hand, you can use hexdec() to reformat a hexadecimal value to decimal and use octdec() to reformat an octal value to decimal.

You might think of converting hex to oct or vice versa. Unfortunately, PHP does not have constructs like hexoct() or octhex(). To perform that kind of operation, you will need to manually convert the integer to decimal first then convert it to hex or oct.

Float or Double

Floating numbers are real numbers (or approximations of real numbers). In other words, it can contain fractional decimal values.

Since integers are a subset of real numbers, integers are floating numbers. Just adding a decimal point and a zero to an integer in PHP will make PHP consider that the type of the variable that will store that value is float instead of integer.

Boolean

Boolean is composed of two values: True and False. In PHP, true and false are not case sensitive. Both values are used primarily in conditional statements, just like in JavaScript.

Also, false is equivalent to null, a blank string, and 0 while true is equivalent to any number except 0 or any string that contains at least one character.

NULL

This is a special value type. In case that a variable does not contain a value from any other data types, it will have a NULL value instead. For example, if you try to access a property from an object that has not been assigned a value yet, it will have a NULL value. By the way, you can assign NULL to variables, too.

Resource

Resources is a special variable type. They only serve as a reference to external resource and are only created by special functions. An example of a resource is a database link.

Chapter 5: Data Types – Part 2

The data types explained in this chapter are essential to your PHP programming life. In other programming languages, you can live without this data types. However, in PHP, you will encounter them most of the time, especially if you will start to learn and use databases on your scripts.

ARRAYS

Arrays are data containers for multiple values. You can store numbers, strings, and even arrays in an array. Array in PHP is a tad different in JavaScript, so it will be discussed in detail in this book.

There are three types of array in PHP: indexed, associative, and multidimensional.

Indexed Arrays

Indexed array is the simplest form of arrays in PHP. For those people who are having a hard time understanding arrays, think of an array as a numbered list that starts with zero. To create or assign values to an array, you must use the construct array(). For example:

```php
<?php
$examplearray = array(1, 2, "three");
?>
```

To call values inside an array, you must call them using their respective indices. For example:

```php
<?php
$examplearray = array(1, 2, "three");
echo $examplearray[0];
echo $examplearray['2'];
?>
```

The first echo will reply with 1 and the second echo will reply three. As you can see, in indexed arrays, you can call values with just a number or a number inside quotes. When dealing with indexed arrays, it is best that you use the first method.

Since the number 1 was the first value to be assigned to the array, index 0 was assigned to it. The index number of the values in an array increment by 1. So, the index numbers of the values 2 and three are 1 and 2 respectively.

Associative Arrays

The biggest difference between associative arrays and indexed arrays is that you can define the index keys of the values in associative arrays. The variable $GLOBALS is one of the best example of associative arrays in PHP. To create an associative array, follow the example:

```php
<?php
$examplearray = array("index0" => "John", 2 => "Marci");
echo $examplearray["index0"];
echo $examplearray[2];
?>
```

The first echo will return John and the second echo will return Marci. Take note that if you use associative array, the values will not have indexed numbers.

Multidimensional Arrays

Multidimensional arrays can store values, indexed arrays, and associative arrays. If you create an array in your script, the $GLOBALS variable will become a multidimensional array. You can insert indexed or associative arrays in multidimensional arrays. However, take note that the same rules apply to their index keys. To create one, follow the example below:

```php
<?php
$examplearray = array(array("test1", 1, 2), array("test2" => 3, "test3" => 4), array("test4", 5, 6));
echo $examplearray[1]["test2"];
echo $examplearray[1][1];
echo $examplearray[2][0];
?>
```

As you can see, creating multidimensional arrays is just like nesting arrays on its value. Calling values from multidimensional is simple.

If a value was assigned, it can be called like a regular array value using its index key. If a value was paired with a named key, it can be called by its name. If an array was assigned, you can call the value inside it by calling the index key of the array first, and then the index key of the value inside it.

In the example, the third echo called the array in index 2 and accessed the value located on its 0 index. Hence, it returned test4.

Objects

Objects are like small programs inside your script. You can assign variables within them called properties. You can also assign functions within them called methods.

Creating and using objects can make you save hundreds of lines of code, especially if you have some bundle of codes that you need to use repeatedly on your scripts. To be on the safe side, the advantages of using objects depend on the situation and your preferences.

Debates about using objects in their scripts (object oriented programming) or using functions (procedural programming) instead have been going on forever. It is up to you if you will revolve your programs around objects or not.

Nevertheless, to create objects, you must create a class for them first. Below is an example on how to create a class in PHP.

```php
<?php
class Posts {
        function getPost() {
                $this->post1 = "Post Number 1.";
        }
        var $post2 = "Post Number 2.";
}

$test = new Posts();
echo $test->post2;
$test->getPost();
echo $test->post1;
?>
```

In this example, a new class was created using the class keyword. The name of the class being created is Posts. In class declarations, you can create functions that will be methods for the objects under the class. And you can create variables that will be properties for the subjects under the class.

First, a function was declared. If the function was called, it will create a property for an object under the Posts class called post1. Also, a value was assigned to it. You might have noticed the $this part in the declaration inside the function. The $this variable represents the object that owns the function being declared.

Besides it is a dash and a chevron (->). Some programmers informally call it as the instance operator. This operator allows access to the instances (methods and properties) of an object. In the statement, the script is accessing the post1 property inside the $this object, which is the object that owns the function. After accessing the property, the statement assigned a value to it.

Aside from the function or method declaration, the script created a property called post2, which is a variable owned by the Posts class. To declare one, you need to use the keyword var (much like in JavaScript). After this statement, the class declaration ends.

The next statement contains the variable assignment, $test = new Posts(). Technically, that means that the variable $test will become a new object under the Posts class. All the methods and properties that was declared inside the Posts() class declaration will be given to it.

To test if the $test class became a container for a Posts object, the script accessed the property post2 from $test and then echoed it to produce an output. The echo will return , 'Post number 2.'. Indeed, the $test variable is already an object under the Posts class.

What if you call and print the property post1 from the variable $test? It will not return anything since it has not been created or initialized yet. To make it available, you need to invoke the getPost() method of $test. Once you do, you will be able to access the property post1.

And that is just the tip of the iceberg. You will be working more on objects on advanced PHP projects.

Conclusion

Thank you again for purchasing this book!

I hope this book was able to help you to learn PHP fast.

The next step is to:

Learn the other superglobals

Learn from handling in HTML, JavaScript, and PHP

Learn using MySQL

Finally, if you enjoyed this book, please take the time to share your thoughts and post a review on Amazon. We do our best to reach out to readers and provide the best value we can. Your positive review will help us achieve that. It'd be greatly appreciated!

Thank you and good luck!

Check Out My Other Books

Below you'll find some of my other popular books that are popular on Amazon and Kindle as well. Simply click on the links below to check them out. Alternatively, you can visit my author page on Amazon to see other work done by me.

Android Programming in a Day

Python Programming in a Day

C Programming Success in a Day

CSS Programming Professional Made Easy

C Programming Professional Made Easy

JavaScript Programming Made Easy

Windows 8 Tips for Beginners

Windows 8 Tips for Beginners

HTML Professional Programming Made Easy

C ++ Programming Success in a Day

If the links do not work, for whatever reason, you can simply search for these titles on the Amazon website to find them.

www.ingramcontent.com/pod-product-compliance
Lightning Source LLC
Chambersburg PA
CBHW061047050326
40689CB00012B/3000